D0686926

All About Branches of the U.S. Military

THE UNITED STATES
AIR FORCE

by Tracy Vonder Brink

PEBBLE
a capstone imprint

Pebble Explore is published by Pebble, an imprint of Capstone.
1710 Roe Crest Drive, North Mankato, Minnesota 56003
www.capstonepub.com

Library of Congress Cataloging-in-Publication Data
Names: Vonder Brink, Tracy, author.
Title: The United States Air Force / by Tracy Vonder Brink.
Description: North Mankato, Minnesota : Pebble, [2021] | Series: All about branches of the U.S. military | Includes bibliographical references and index. | Audience: Ages 6-8 (provided by Capstone) | Audience: Grades 2-3 (provided by Capstone)
Identifiers: LCCN 2020025155 (print) | LCCN 2020025154 (ebook) | ISBN 9781977131720 (hardcover) | ISBN 9781977155054 (pdf) | ISBN 9781977156679 (kindle)
Subjects: LCSH: United States. Air Force--Juvenile literature.
Classification: LCC UG633 .V66 2021 (ebook) | LCC UG633 (print) | DDC 358.400973--dc23
LC record available at https://lccn.loc.gov/2020025155

Summary: Describes basics of the United States Air Force, including its aircraft, missions, and the jobs of airmen.

Image Credits
U.S. Air Force photo by Airman 1st Class Ashley Wood, 15, Airman 1st Class Levin Boland, 28, Airman 1st Class Michael S. Murphy, 5 (Bottom), Airman 1st Class Tara Stetler, 23 (Top), Airman 1st Class Valerie Seelye, 7, Airman 1st Class William Rio Rosado, 24, Capt. Kip Sumner, 17, Joshua Armstrong, 27 (Bottom), Master Sgt. Donald R. Allen, 19 (Bottom), Master Sgt. Eric Harris, 29, Master Sgt. Mark C. Olsen, 5 (Top), Melinda Mueller, 8, Senior Airman Ericka Engblom, 23 (Bottom), Senior Airman Luke Milano, 10, Staff Sgt. Angelita M. Lawrence, 27 (Top), Staff Sgt. Chris Drzazgowski, 20, Staff Sgt. Jerry Morrison, 21, Staff Sgt. Rasheen Douglas, 13 (Bottom), Tech. Sgt. Carlin Leslie, Cover, 1, Tech. Sgt. Liliana Moreno, 11, Tech. Sgt. Ned T. Johnston, 19 (Top), Tommie Horton, 13 (Top), U.S. Air Force Public Affairs, 25; U.S. Air National Guard photo by Senior Airman John Linzmeier, 9

Design Elements
Capstone; Shutterstock: CRVL, Zerbor

Editorial Credits
Editor: Carrie Sheely; Designer: Kayla Rossow; Media Researcher: Jo Miller; Production Specialist: Laura Manthe

All internet sites appearing in back matter were available and accurate when this book was sent to press.

Table of Contents

Words in **bold** are in the glossary.

WHAT IS THE AIR FORCE?

Whoosh! An F-22 Raptor plane flies through the sky. Its big engines sound like thunder. It's just one of the many amazing planes of the United States Air Force.

The Air Force is a branch of the U.S. **military**. It started in 1947. Its members fight in the sky. More than 300,000 people are in the Air Force. They are called airmen.

F-22 Raptor

JOINING THE AIR FORCE

Men and women can join the Air Force. They must be 17 to 39 years old. They must be healthy and fit. U.S. **citizens** can join. Some noncitizens living lawfully in the U.S. can also join.

Airmen can be active duty or in the Air Force Reserve. Active-duty airmen have full-time jobs. Those in the Reserve usually work part-time.

Airmen go to a school for basic training. It takes nearly nine weeks. The airmen exercise. They learn about guns and other **weapons**. They learn to work together.

Airmen put up a tent in basic training.

After basic training, each airman gets a job. There are more than 200 kinds of jobs. Some become **pilots**. They fly aircraft. Others are in charge of supplies. Some fix planes.

Active-duty airmen work at Air Force bases. A base is like a town for airmen. They live on or near the base. Their families can live with them.

Sometimes airmen are **deployed** on **missions**. They might fight in another country. They might help after a storm or other natural disaster. They must leave their home base. Their families stay behind. These missions can last for up to a year.

AIR FORCE UNIFORMS AND GEAR

Airmen wear different uniforms. The combat uniform is one. Airmen wear it to fight. They often wear it on bases. Airmen wear other uniforms at special events.

Airmen wear a flight suit for flying in planes. It keeps them comfortable. They can wear a one-piece or a two-piece suit.

combat uniforms

flight suits

A fighter plane pilot wears a g-suit. These planes speed up quickly. The force of **gravity** pushes against a pilot's body. The force can cause blood to rush down from the pilot's brain. This can make the pilot **pass out**. The suit keeps the pilot safe.

Fighter planes fly very high. The air is thin there. It is hard to breathe. Fighter pilots wear special masks. The masks give them more air.

The mask is part of a helmet. It has a radio inside. It lets pilots talk to other airmen. Some helmets even show information like a computer screen does. It might show a map.

AIR FORCE AIRCRAFT

The Air Force has many aircraft. Each is built for a job. Some are used to fight battles. Some carry supplies. Others take pictures. Some fly in air shows.

The F-35A Lightning is a fast fighter plane. It can fly 1,200 miles (1,931 kilometers) per hour. It can fight enemy planes. It can drop **bombs** to hit ground **targets**. The F-35A is a **stealth** plane. It is hard for enemies to find.

Air Force F-16 planes in an air show

F-35A Lightning

The F-22 Raptor is another stealth fighter. It is even faster than the F-35A! It flies about 1,500 miles (2,400 km) per hour. It can make very sharp turns.

F-22 Raptor

A KC-10 refuels a plane.

Fighter planes take long flights. They might not be able to land for fuel. The KC-10 Extender plane is like a gas station in the sky. A fighter plane flies up to it. A tube connects the planes. Fuel goes from the KC-10 to the other plane.

The Air Force also has cargo planes. They carry people and supplies. The C-17 Globemaster is one. It is very big. It can hold 170,900 pounds (77,519 kilograms) of cargo. It can carry more than 100 people. Its back opens. Vehicles can drive right into it!

Unmanned Aerial Vehicles (UAVs) don't have any people inside. Airmen control them from the ground. One is the MQ-9 Reaper. Airmen can fly it from 1,150 miles (1,851 km) away. It can take pictures. It can drop bombs.

MQ-9 Reaper

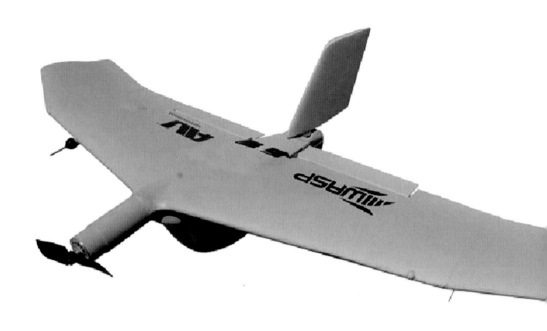

The Wasp UAV weighs less than 3 pounds (1.4 kg). It carries cameras. Airmen can fly it from up to 3 miles (5 km) away.

LIFE IN THE AIR FORCE

An airman's day depends on his or her job. Airmen go to their jobs on the base during the week. They exercise often. They may have free time in the evenings and on weekends.

Airmen keep learning in their jobs. Pilots fly on practice missions. They learn about new planes. They test new gear. They need to be ready for missions.

Airmen stay in the Air Force between four and eight years. Some join again. Over time, airmen can rise in **rank**. Some become officers. Officers are in charge of other airmen.

Airmen load up food to help people in Haiti.

Airmen are always ready to serve. They may need to fight. They may need to bring supplies to places wrecked by disasters. The brave men and women of the Air Force will continue to protect the United States from the sky.

GLOSSARY

bomb (BAHM)—an object filled with explosives that blow up

citizen (SI-tuh-zuhn)—a member of a country or state who has the right to live there

deploy (di-PLOY)—to move troops into position for military action

gravity (GRAV-uh-tee)—a force that pulls objects with mass together; gravity pulls objects down toward the center of Earth

military (MIL-uh-ter-ee)—the armed forces of a country

mission (MISH-uhn)—a military task

pass out (PAS AUT)—to lose consciousness, or to no longer be aware of what is happening around you

pilot (PYE-luht)—a person who flies a plane

rank (RAYNK)—an official position or job level

stealth (STELTH)—having the ability to move secretly

target (TAR-git)—an object at which to aim or shoot

weapon (WEP-uhn)—something that can be used in a fight to attack or defend

READ MORE

Boothroyd, Jennifer. *Inside the U.S. Air Force.* Minneapolis: Lerner Publishing Group, 2017.

Caulkins, Sam. *My Uncle Is in the Air Force.* New York: PowerKids Press, 2016.

Cooke, Tim. *A Timeline of Fighter Jets and Bomber Planes.* North Mankato, MN: Capstone Press, 2018.

INTERNET SITES

The Conversation: Curious Kids: What's It Like to Be a Fighter Pilot?
theconversation.com/curious-kids-whats-it-like-to-be-a-fighter-pilot-100563

Ducksters: U.S. Government: United States Armed Forces
www.ducksters.com/history/us_government/united_states_armed_forces.php

Kiddle: United States Air Force Facts for Kids
kids.kiddle.co/United_States_Air_Force

INDEX